THIS IS

LOVE

ACCORDING TO GOD'S WILL

HMPH. YOU'RE ONE OF
THOSE CHRISTIANS

MIMI EMMANUEL

The Truth, Love & God series (1)

THIS IS LOVE ACCORDING TO GOD'S WILL

The Truth, Love & God series (1)

All my books are written for my children, grandchildren and my Godchild.

HOW TO LOVE ACCORDING TO GOD'S WILL - THIS IS LOVE!

PLEASE NOTE: *'How to Love According to God's Will''* has come about after a couple of decades of Bible study and introspection. Various pastors, priests and ministers have been consulted and up until recently every single one vehemently disagrees with my findings. I have been excommunicated by the Catholic Church and am now officially a heretic.

The above credentials are the best that I can come up with.

Another *Sola Scriptura* publication from Mosaic House Co.

Various public domain Bible translations such as the King James and Literal Translation, have been utilised for the Scripture quoted in *'How To Love According to God's Will.'* We thank the Bible translators who made GOD's Word freely available to us all through the public domain. For my research I use multiple other resources including Jewish Bible, JPS Hebrew-English, Strong's Exhaustive Concordance of the Bible, The Brown-Driver-Briggs Hebrew and Eglish Lexikon and more as can be found on this link, which lists some of my favourite Biblical resources,

https://liveforeverhowto.wordpress.com/2016/05/06/15-of-my-best-and-favourite-biblical-resources

All Scriptural references are provided so that readers can do their own research using their preferred Bible translation. To get the message across succinctly for readers who are not familiar with the Bible, occasionally I've paraphrased

Scripture 'the Aussie way.' This may not be politically correct but is done to improve the readability of this study.

For the full story download a free Bible.

Mosaic House Co.
Post box 25 Noosa
Queensland 4567
Australia

Or visit us at www.mosaichouse.co.

With special thanks to Red Hat Inc.

ISBN: 978-1-925944-07-5

Made in the Commonwealth of Australia.

The Truth, Love & God series (1)

Published in the United States of America

Cover design by A Emmanuel

Layout and formatting by SunnyEdesign

Editor Elaine Roughton

written in 2009 and published in 2018 – ©myemmanuel

If I read correctly, the premise for your book is that we show we love God by keeping His commandments. That we serve a perfect God but the imperfection of people means that God's Word and His laws are interpreted in many different ways.

This is true! Jesus did not come to abolish the law, He came to fulfil it. As in Matthew 5:17.

Loving the Lord our God with all our heart, with all our soul, with all our strength and with all our mind and love our neighbour as ourselves (Luke 10:27) means that the desire and choice to keep His commandments will be a natural flow-on from this. .

We want to be obedient to Him; we want to do His will and the commandments are there to show us what His will is. They are a way we can respond to Him. We need to be responding to Him. God is a God of love and mercy but also justice. He disciplines and corrects us as He sees fit, all the while to help us conform to the likeness of His Son Jesus.

We do fall short, all the time, as Christians. But we keep on going and doing our best to serve God the way He has decreed. And the gift of grace that Jesus gave us keeps covering us as we continue on, as we genuinely seek to do His will. To honour Him and obey Him.

I like the way you have presented the book as a response to a "typical" person who is not a Christian.

I like the way you invite the reader to be discerning, to investigate and read the Scriptures provided about what God's will is.

Meredith Swift

Biblical references for *Book One: How to Love According to God's Will; This is Love*, can be downloaded from this link.

https://mailchi.mp/c2778452b3c8/tg1ref

Read my special note here.

The Truth, Love & God series (1)

DEDICATION

"Don't be like Cain, who belonged to that evil one, and killed his brother. And why did he kill him? Because his own deeds were evil, and his brother's work was good." (1 John 3:12, also Matthew 5:21-22)

This book is for you, Brad. And for your friends.

The Truth, Love & God series (1)

CONTENTS

1. What is Love?
Does the Bible Tell Us?

Come, children, listen to me;

I will teach you reverence for the LORD.

(Psalm 34:11)

Is Christianity a hoax? Let's get real about what it means to walk as He walked. Cause that's what Christians claim to do. They claim to follow Jesus Christ, who was born between 6 and 4 BC, in Bethlehem. He grew up in Nazareth, preached around AD 27–29, and was crucified around AD 30 or 36. Jesus said that His disciples can be recognised by the love they have for each other and that He was born to give witness to the truth.

Jesus' life, His story, and that of His ancestors is told in the Bible.

The King James translation of the Bible mentions the word 'love' or a variation thereof 442 times. Love is important.

It is the most important as well as the most misunderstood message in the Bible.

Everybody talks about how much God loves us and that He sent His own son (Jesus) to earth to save us.

This is true.

But what about us loving God? Our Father can love us for all He likes, if we don't respond, we're toast.

All over the world people are killing each other in the name of God. Does He want us to do that? That's a no, for sure!

People tell me that under the new covenant all we need to do is, 'love each other.' But how?

How do we love according to God's will so that we may have access to the myriad of blessings and promises made in the Bible?

God has explicitly set out in His Holy Word how He would like us to love Him back.

Let's find out.

2. Religion is the Cause of Hatred

He interrupted my thoughts as he was hitting away at my tap. 'Bang, bang, bang,' the sound made my ears sting. I stopped writing.

He accidentally dropped a washer down the gurgler. At the same time he exclaimed;

I HATE RELIGION!

"I HATE religion!"

"Why is that?" I asked, wondering if it was <u>stuff in the news</u> or the Scripture verses on my walls triggering that comment.

"*As for me and my house, we will serve The Lord.*"

Joshua 24:14

"Because religion is the cause of most of the wars and hatred in the world," my newfound friend Brad said.

I asked him if he really believed that, and without even thinking about it, he shot back at me, "I do not believe it, I'm convinced of it!"

"All religions?" I asked him.

Without hesitation, he responded, "ALL of them."

I said, "Funny that, because my religion tells me that we are to love each other."

"What religion would that be?" he quizzed.

"I love God's Word," I said.

3. "Mmpphh, You're One of Those Christians"

"Mmpphh, you're one of those Christians," He said.

Clearly, Brad was assuming things. What was I to say to that? I did not know what he meant when he said, 'one of those,' but I wanted him to like me and not hate me because of my religion.

But more than that, I wanted to get across to him that my religion is one of love.

I was not quite sure how to go about that because, Brad clearly had preconceived notions about Christianity, and what entails being a Christian, or being someone that loves God's Word.

I didn't know what his preconceived ideas were, other than that they weren't positive.

The Truth, Love & God series (1)

4. "I Love God's Word"

So I repeated what is true for me and said, "I love God's Word."

Brad came over and sat down next to me. "You mean the Bible, don't you?"

I nodded affirmatively.

Well, that really got him going. He stood up again and walked up and down my living room with the spanner in his left hand, waving his arms up and down in despair.

"The Bible has caused more wars and deaths and calamity than all other religions combined! How anyone can believe in fairy tales like that is beyond me."

Maybe it was premature when earlier I referred to Brad as my newfound friend. My daughter had brought him over to fix a couple of leaky taps and a gate that had come off its hinges.

I treated him as a friend because I was grateful that he came to fix a few things for a reasonable fee, but I do not like it when people refer to God's Holy Word as fairy tales.

Over time I've learned to recognise that this reference is generally used by people who have never read God's Word.

I did not want him to go on a rant of no return. For the sake of our now seemingly fragile friendship, I decided to find out what got him going like that.

"You seem pretty passionate about your anti-religion stance, Brad. Where is that coming from?"

He sat down next to me again. "Mimi, come on, you can see what's going on in the world, surely?"

5. "If it Weren't for Religion…"

"If it weren't for religion…"

His voice trailed off, and as he was about to take in a breath of fresh air, I noted,"Religion doesn't do anything, Brad. It's people and their interpretation of religion that can be a problem."

He got up again, down. Up once more. He sure was passionate about the subject.

"So Mimi, you're saying that the Bible doesn't tell people to kill each other if they don't believe according to the teachings?"

Before I could answer, he continued. "You do know about the Inquisition and all the 'Holy Wars' that have been raging throughout the ages?"

The Truth, Love & God series (1)

6. Do You Know About the Inquisition?

"Yes, I do Brad," I said.

And then I asked him, "Do you know about God's will for his people; His Commandments?"

Brad shook his head as he walked back to the tap.

"What do they have to do with anything," he asked. "Does anyone even care about those anymore?"

"Good question, Brad, and pertinent too. You're absolutely right. For all sorts of different reasons, lots of 'believers' indeed think that these Commandments don't apply to them. They argue old covenant versus new covenant. But what it boils down to is that many are of the opinion that their faith sets them above the law."

The Truth, Love & God series (1)

7. Do You Know About the Commandments?

"To get back to your other questions, Brad, yes, I know about the Inquisition and all the 'Holy Wars,' and as far as I'm concerned the Commandments have everything to do with this. And you know why?"

He stood there looking at me, not quite sure where the conversation was going. So I continued.

"I tell you why the Commandments matter. They matter because the Commandments tell us not to kill, not to steal, not to lie, not to commit adultery, not to covet, to respect our elders, and so on. This is God's will for us. This is what God's Word teaches us right from the very beginning.

The Commandments set a moral standard for the whole of society.

We were taught to be nice to our neighbours and to treat foreigners with kindness, and the Bible tells us that those simple ten rules constitute love. They are a benchmark, a measure to live by and live up to."

Brad looked at me and said, "Sounds wonderful, Mimi. Here's a reality check for you, NO one is paying any attention or listening to any of those rules, nor following them."

8. People Interpret God's Word Any Way They Like

"Exactly my point, Brad. It isn't for me to judge if anyone is following God's will; what I notice, however, is that many believers follow all kinds of rules set by their church and community, but not necessarily The Ten. Wouldn't it be wonderful indeed if we were to follow those ten simple rules? There's nothing wrong with those rules, is there?"

Brad shrugged, seemingly in agreement.

I continued. "There's nothing wrong with the Bible, either."

What's wrong is that all through the ages, and still today, people interpret God's Word any way they like to suit their own purposes.

The Bible tells us to love one another. God showed His love for us by sending His own Son down to earth to teach us about true love.

We're taught that Jesus' disciples will be known for their love for each other, we're encouraged to turn the other cheek, bless our enemies, and we're taught that God is love, and if we do not love we do not have God in us. Can you find fault with any of that, Brad?"

Brad looked bewildered. "But, Mimi, no one is DOING that 'loving thing.' All these so called religious people are killing each other!"

"I know that Brad," I said. "Does that make the Commandments wrong, or the people?"

9. What are These Again, the Commandments?

Brad scratched his head as he asked; "What are these again, the Commandments?"

So, Brad, my friend, this is for you.

God's Commandments

And he gave Moses, when he finished talking with him on Mount Sinai, two tables of testimony, tables of stone, written with the finger of God. (Exodus 31:18)

… Listen to all the words and close them in your hearts and command your children to do and keep all the words of this law.

This is not a small thing; it is your life… (Deuteronomy 32:46-47)

One

I am God, YHVH, who saved you.

Only respect and admire me (what is good) and not evil. No other gods.

Two

Don't create images or likenesses of anything that is in heaven above, or in the earth beneath, nor of those things that are in the waters under the earth.

Don't admire nor serve them. You and your children and your children's children will be in trouble if you do. I will show mercy unto thousands that love me, and keep my commandments.

Three

Don't take my name in vain.

You'll be punished if you do.

Four

Remember to keep one day a week holy; the Sabbath day. You'll work six days, but the seventh day is the Sabbath of the Lord thy God. Don't work on that day. Not you, nor your son, nor your daughter, nor your employee or servant, nor your animals that live with you.

For in six days the Lord made heaven and earth, and the sea, and all things that are in them, and rested on the seventh day: therefore the Lord blessed the seventh day, and sanctified it.

Five

Respect your mum and dad;

that you may live long.

Six

Don't kill.

Seven

Don't commit adultery.

Eight

Don't steal.

Nine

Don't lie.

Ten

Don't covet.

This is love

This commandment that I give you today is certainly not too difficult or not possible for you to keep. (Deuteronomy 30:11)

This is the love of God, that we keep his commandments: and his commandments are not hard to keep. (1 John 5:3)

Forever settled in heaven

Forever, O LORD, Your word is settled in heaven. (Psalm 119:89)

As we can see, the love of God is that we keep His Commandments, which aren't hard to keep. These Commandments are settled in heaven forever. If anyone tells you any different; this is not in line with Scripture, but likely to come out of a Pharisee's mouth. You know, one of those Pharisees that Jesus warned us against.

Blessings and promises

In addition, the Commandments contain blessings and promises.

The first promise is a promise of trouble for those who violate the second Commandment.

The second promise is that mercy will be shown to those who love God and keep His Commandments.

The third promise is one of punishment for those who take God's name in their mouth for no good reason.

The seventh day of the week is designated as a rest day for God's people and Our Father blessed this day.

Then there's also the promise/blessing of long life for those who honour their elders (Mum and Dad).

10. Does the Bible Tell Us What Love is?

Yes, the Bible tells us what love is and how to love according to God's will.

God is love and He tells us that not lying, killing, stealing, etc., constitutes love.

You can watch this video, 'What Is Love?' to see what love is according to the prophets… from the very beginning from Mount Sinai. See References for link.

Did Jesus agree with the prophets?

Jesus came and gave his own sermon from a mount early in his ministry, believed to have been on the northwestern shore of the Sea of Galilee, between Capernaum and Gennesaret (Ginosar), on the southern slopes of the Korazim Plateau.

This sermon is also referred to as, 'The Sermon on the Mount' and 'The Beatitudes' because of the blessings it contains. You can find this sermon in The Gospel of Matthew, chapters 5, 6 and 7.

This is where Jesus said, 'You've been told not to kill. I say hatred is as bad; turn the

31

other cheek. Forgive so that you will be forgiven.

You've been told not to commit adultery; I tell you lusting after someone is as bad.

You've been told not to covet, I'm telling you that if you have two garments, to give one of them away. Don't worry about tomorrow, our Father will take care of you.

You've been told not to swear, I tell you that calling someone a fool will get you in BIG TROUBLE with the BIG BOSS.'

Jesus was not only in total agreement with the Commandments (the law that Moses spoke about), but lived accordingly and expected his followers to do the same.

Live like Jesus

Whosoever claims to be like Jesus must live the way He lived. (1 John 2:6)

Is Christianity a hoax? Yes, it is if you call yourself a Christian and claim to live like Jesus and you don't.

Christians are supposed to be pulling each other up, not dumbing each other down. We know that Moses told us about the law and Jesus told us about grace. It's not one or the other. As Jesus showed us, it is both.

For there to be grace, there had to be a law first.

Law as well as grace

The law was given by Moses;
grace and truth came through Jesus Christ.
(John 1:17)

People say, "but we 'try' to be good." Sure, we all know what the road to hell is paved with.

I write about this all the time because I am passionate that God's Word does not get corrupted but is truthfully presented.

Yes, the Bible tells us what Love is. Our love for the Most High and our fellow human beings manifests when we make genuine efforts to live according to his Commandments and according to His will.

His grace, mercy, and love, for those who respect and fear Him, is beyond our comprehension.

Great mercy

He does not treat us as we deserve
according to our bad behaviour nor do we
get repaid according to our evil deeds. But
as high as the heavens are above the earth,

so great is His mercy and love towards those that fear and respect Him. (Psalm 103:10-11, Luke 1:50)

11. Scripture Verses About God's Will

What is God's will?

Below are Scripture verses that tell us about God's will.

Do God's will and live forever

The world and all its desires is passing away,
but anyone who does God's will shall live forever. (1 John 2:17)

Do God's will to be related to Jesus

Whoever does the will of God,
is my brother, my sister, and mother. (Mark 3:35)

Teach me to do your will

Teach me to do your will; for thou art my God: thy spirit is good; lead me into the land of uprightness. (Psalm 143:10)

Do my Father's will to enter the kingdom

Not every one that saith unto me, Lord, Lord, shall enter into the kingdom of heaven; but he that doeth the will of my Father which is in heaven. (Matthew 7:21)

For I have come down from heaven, not to do My own will, but to do the will of Him who sent Me.

And this is the will of Him who sent Me, that I shall lose none of those He has given Me, but raise them up at the last day.

For it is My Father's will that everyone who looks to the Son and believes in Him shall have eternal life, and I will raise him up at the last day." (John 6:38-40)

Do His will to understand the Truth

If any man will do His will, he shall know of the doctrine, whether it be of God, or whether I speak of myself. (John 7:17)

The Lord reveals His Covenant

The LORD confides in those who fear Him, and reveals His covenant to them. (Psalm 25:14)

Have God's law in your heart

I delight to do your will, O my God; your law is within my heart. (Psalm 40:8)

God listens to those who do His will

We know that God does not listen to sinners (those who break His Commandments), but if anyone is a worshiper of God and does His will, God listens to him. (John 9:31)

My nourishment comes from doing God's will

Then Jesus said: "My food comes from doing the will of God (My Father), who sent me, and from finishing his work. (John 4:34)

God's will written with His own finger

*I will give you the tablets
with the law and the commandments
which I have written on stone
with my own finger for
the instruction of my people;
'If ye love me, keep my commandments.'
(Exodus 24:12, 31:18, John 14:15)*

More promises

The above Scripture verses tell us that eternal life is promised to those who do God's will.

We become part of God's family when we do His will and Jesus becomes our brother.

Living according to God's will leads us into the promised land, the kingdom of heaven.

Jesus, our mentor, tells us that we're on this earth to live according to God's will, not our own.

It is our Father's will that we live according to Jesus' teachings. When we live as He told us, we are promised eternal life.

We'll understand Scripture when we do God's will because our Father will confide in us when we live according to His will and He will reveal His covenant to us.

Doing God's will means that we have God's law in our heart and our Father will listen to us when we call upon Him.

When we live according to God's will, we'll help finish God's work and this nourishes us.

God's own finger wrote in stone instructions (His will) for His people, never to be forgotten; *'show your love for me by keeping my commandments.'*

People who love God make a genuine effort to keep His commandments.

More on the 'love theme'

Here is a link to another blog post on the 'love theme.'

It's from my liveforeverhowto.wordpress.com blog and called; 'Is Heaven just for Jesus' friends?' See References for link.

12. AFTERWORD

*So shall he sprinkle many nations…
for that which had not been told them
shall they see; and that which they had not
heard shall they consider.
(Isaiah 52:15)*

After I started reading the Bible, I became keen to find out about God's purpose for my life. After some time I realised that God's will is the same for all of us.

And His will for us is to be a true reflection of Himself and His Son which means to be a kind and loving, compassionate person with a warm heart.

The how-to can be found in the Ten Rules written with God's own finger in stone, never to be forgotten or abolished.

The finer details and individual nuances come to us through inner promptings, insights and urges and even dreams that reveal God's bigger plan to us as we mature and as He draws us closer and closer to Him.

I was dismayed to find out that many churches teach that 'the Commandments have been done away with.'

This is not what Jesus taught. Jesus followed the Commandments during His life. We are told that He didn't sin. This means that He never broke any of the Commandments.

Which made me wonder, Is Christianity just a hoax? Aren't we told to follow in His footsteps?

Use your own discretion when you hear someone say that, what God's own finger wrote in stone does not apply any longer. Or if someone tells you that, yes, Jesus followed the Commandments but we don't have to.

Don't believe anyone's message, including mine, without investigating for yourself. Read what the Father and His Son say about following their rules. They set the standard and are the benchmark.

My words dear within your heart

Hold my words dear within your heart...
"I will put my law in their minds
and write it on their hearts."
(Deuteronomy 11:18, Jeremiah 31:33)

Pray and follow your heart.

May God bless your journey. I pray that my readers will enjoy a loving and peaceful life.

Mimi

The Truth, Love & God series (1)

The Truth, Love & God Series

The *Truth, Love & God* series came about after Mimi realised that the 'Jesus stories' told by her Mum were true. As in, Jesus was not just a mythical figure but a real person, the Son of God, who had come down to earth to save humanity from itself.

This realisation prompted years of Bible study and reflection, as well as amazement at how Jesus' sacrifice is still not fully understood and His love hardly ever truly appreciated and reciprocated.

The *Truth, Love & God* series looks into the truth about God and Jesus' love for humanity and how we are reciprocating. And few of us ever respond in kind, really. I certainly know that I take their love for granted most of the time.

This is in gratitude and with regret for my lackadaisical response to the love that has been lavished on me and my family by our Father and His Son; the love of my life. Without you I am nothing.

Written for my children, grandchildren and my Godson.

Book One -

How To Live According To God's Will: This is Love! - "Mpphh You're one of those Christians!"
Is Christianity a hoax? Let's get real about Christianity
We're supposed to be pulling each other up, not dumbing each other down.

Coming up:

Book Two

WHAT IS TRUE LOVE? ACCORDING TO THE BIBLE: "Love is when your name is safe in someone's mouth." What does 'loving the Christian way' mean? Is it different from mainstream loving?

Sign up here to find out when Book Two in the Truth, Love & God Series; 'What Is True Love? According To The Bible,' will be published.

Thank you for leaving a review on Amazon if you enjoyed, 'How to Love According to God's Will? - This is Love! By Mimi Emmanuel

Excerpt from My Next Book

What is True Love? According to The Bible

How to describe love

One of the nicest ways I've heard love described was by a little child. When the 7-year-old was asked what she thought love was all about, she wrinkled her nose and stated with authority that, 'Love is when your name is safe in someone's mouth.'

Love is when your name is safe in someone's mouth.

I'll definitely go with that one and will do my very best to keep everyone's name safe in my mouth. Without a doubt that is what Jesus meant when he reiterated His Father's' Word and said that we are to love each other and not to speak idle words or call anyone a fool.

What does the Holy Word say about love?

To get a better handle on the whole loving and relationship thing I decided to find out more in-depth what our Creator and His Son have to say about love. What I noticed is that we are 'commanded' to love each other.

I used to think that, well you know, some people we love and others we don't. Simply because some people are lovable and others aren't. Not so, according to Scripture; just get over yourselves and love each other already.

Many of us aren't that keen on anything unfamiliar, but our Father tells us to,

"Love the stranger like ourselves."

Talk is cheap. The Bible tells us to take care of each other. Period. Later on I'll give you real life examples of true love.

END OF Excerpt

Biblical References

https://mailchi.mp/c2778452b3c8/tg1ref

DEDICATION

Don't kill

"Don't be like Cain, who belonged to that evil one, and killed his brother. And why did he kill him? Because his own deeds were evil, and his brother's work was good." (1 John 3:12)

Don't murder nor hate

"You have heard that it was said to the people long ago, 'You shall not murder, and anyone who murders will be subject to judgment..'" (Matthew 5:21-22)

The Bible

You can read the Bible in your preferred language and translation by clicking here.

(https://www.biblegateway.com/versions) Courtesy of Bible Gateway and the various publishing companies.

You can listen to God's Holy Word online here.
(https://www.biblegateway.com/passage/?search=genesis+1&version=KJV) Courtesy of Bible Gateway and reader Max McLean.

To get a hard copy of the Bible you can walk into any church where they will readily provide you with one, or you can download a Bible app here (https://www.youversion.com/the-bible-app/) or here (https://www.bible.com/app) and read your preferred version in your favourite format.

For my research I use various Bibles and resources. Here is a link

(https://liveforeverhowto.wordpress.com/2016/05/06/15-of-my-best-and-favourite-biblical-resources) to a write-up about my best and favourite Bible resources.

Free download to references

The Biblical references for 'How to Live According to God's Will - This is Love!' Can be downloaded here

https://mailchi.mp/c2778452b3c8/tg1ref

1. What is Love? Does the Bible tell Us?

Come, children, listen to me; I will teach you reverence for the LORD. (Psalm 34:11)

God sent his own Son

God so loved the world that he gave his only begotten Son, that whosoever believeth in him should not perish, but have everlasting life. (John 3:16)

2. Religion is the cause of hatred

Love each other

... love your neighbors as you love yourself... (Leviticus 19:18)

... 'Love your neighbor as yourself.' (Matthew 22:39)

Thou shalt love the Lord thy God with all thy heart, and with all thy soul, and with all thy mind. This is the first and great commandment. And the second is like unto it, Thou shalt love thy neighbour as thyself. On these two commandments hang all the law and the prophets. (Matthew 22:36-40)

3. "Mmpphh, You're One of Those Christians"

If the world hate you, ye know that it hated me before it hated you.

If ye were of the world, the world would love his own: but because ye are not of the world, but I have chosen you out of the world, therefore the world hateth you... If they have persecuted me, they will also persecute you; if they have kept my saying, they will keep yours also.

… He that hateth me hateth my Father also.

… But this cometh to pass, that the word might be fulfilled that is written in their law, They hated me without a cause... (John 15:18-27)

And ye shall be hated of all men for my name's sake: but he that endureth to the end shall be saved. (Matthew 10:22)

Love each other

... love your neighbors as you love yourself… (Leviticus 19:18)

... 'Love your neighbor as yourself.' (Matthew 22:39)

4. I Love God's Word

Scripture of Truth

But I will shew thee that which is noted in the scripture of truth… (Daniel 10:21)

Your word is truth

Sanctify them through your truth: your word is truth. (John 17:17)

5. "If it Weren't for Religion…"

Religion according to the Bible

Pure religion is to help the fatherless and widows and don't get sucked in by the world. (James 1:27)

6. "Do You Know About the Inquisition?"

Which say, Stand by thyself, come not near to me; for I am holier than thou. These are a smoke in my nose, a fire that burneth all the day. (Isaiah 65:5)

…Blessed are you when people insult you, persecute you, and falsely say all kinds of evil against you because of Me. Rejoice and celebrate, because great is your reward in heaven; for in the same way they persecuted the prophets before you. (Matthew 5:11-13)

Rejoice ye in that day, and leap for joy: for, behold, your reward is great in heaven: for in the like manner did their fathers unto the prophets. (Luke 6:23)

7. Do You Know About The Commandments?

The ten rules constitute love

… Love me and keep my commandments (Exodus 20:6)

If ye love me, keep my commandments. (John 14:15)

By this we know that we love the children of God, when we love God, and keep his commandments. (1 John 5:2)

For this is the love of God, that we keep his commandments: and his commandments are not grievous. (1 John 5:3)

And this is love, that we walk after his commandments. This is the commandment, That, as ye have heard from the beginning, ye should walk in it. (2 John 1:6)

Treat foreigners with kindness

Love the foreigner as yourself. (Leviticus 19:34)

… I was a stranger, and you invited me in. (Matthew 25:35)

Follow all kinds of rules

When there was no king in Israel everyone did what was right in his own eyes. (Judges 21:25)

8. People Interpret God's Word Any Way They Like

People interpret God's Word any way they like to suit their own purposes.

For the lips of a priest should preserve knowledge, and people should seek instruction from his mouth, because he is the messenger of the LORD of Hosts." "But you have departed from the way, and your instruction has caused many to stumble. You have violated the covenant of Levi," says the LORD…. (Malachi 2:7-8)

Commandments of men

…They worship Me in vain; they teach as doctrine the rules of men.' You have disregarded the commandment of God to keep the tradition of men." (Mark 7-8)

From the beginning

And this is love, that we walk according to His commandments. This is the very commandment you have heard from the beginning, that you must walk in love. (2 John 1:6)

Jesus' disciples will be known for their love for each other

"… Love one another. As I have loved you, so also you must love one another. By this all men will know that you are My disciples, if you love one another." (John 13:34)

Turn the other cheek

You have heard that it was said, 'Eye for eye and tooth for tooth.' But I tell you not to resist an evil person. If someone slaps you on your right cheek, turn to him the other as well; if someone wants to sue you and take your

*tunic, let him have your cloak as well;…
(Matthew 5:38-40)*

Bless our enemies

*…You have heard that it was said, 'Love your neighbor and hate your enemy.' But I tell you, love your enemies and pray for those who persecute you, that you may be children of your Father in heaven. He causes His sun to rise on the evil and the good, and sends rain on the righteous and the unrighteous…
(Matthew 5:43-45)*

9. What are These Again, the Commandments?

God's Commandments

And he gave Moses, when he finished talking with him on mount Sinai, two tables of testimony, tables of stone, written with the finger of God. (Exodus 31:18)

… Listen to all the words and close them in your hearts and command your children to do and keep all the words of this law.

*This is not a small thing; it is your life…
Deuteronomy (32:46-47)*

1.

I am God, YHVH, who saved you.

Only respect and admire me (what is good) and not evil.

2.

Don't create images or likenesses of anything that is in heaven above, or in the earth beneath,

nor of those things that are

in the waters under the earth.
Don't admire nor serve them.

You and your children and your children's children will be in trouble if you do.

I will show mercy unto thousands that love me, and keep my commandments.

3.

Don't take my name in vain.

You'll be punished if you do.

4.

Remember to keep one day a week holy; the Sabbath day. You'll work six days but the seventh day is the Sabbath of the Lord thy God. Don't work on that day. Not you, nor your son, nor your daughter, nor your employee or servant, nor your animals that live with you.

For in six days the Lord made heaven and earth, and the sea, and all things that are in them, and rested on the seventh day:

therefore the Lord blessed the seventh day, and sanctified it.

5.

Respect your mum and dad;

that you may live long.

6.

Don't kill.

7.

Don't commit adultery.

8.

Don't steal.

9.

Don't lie.

10.

Don't covet.

Life Application

How do I apply this to my life? The Holy Word tells us.

This is love

This commandment that I give you today is certainly not too difficult or not possible for you to keep. Deuteronomy (30:11)

This is the love of God, that we keep his commandments: and his commandments are not hard to keep. (1 John 5:3)

Forever settled in heaven

For ever, O LORD, thy word is settled in heaven. (Psalm 119:89)

Watch out for Pharisees

'Be careful,' Jesus said. 'Watch out for the yeast of the Pharisees and Sadducees.' (Matthew 16:6, see also Luke 11:37–54, Matthew 23:1–39, Mark 12:35–40, Luke 20:45–47)

Pharisees

The Pharisees were a Jewish group of religious leaders mentioned nearly one hundred times in the Gospels. In Biblical times they were the ones supposedly strictly observing the traditional and written law as an example to others. Nowadays they are colloquially known to be hypocrites or people who twist the truth and don't do as they say. Jesus warned against Pharisees repeatedly.

10. Does the Bible Tell Us What Love is?

What is Love? video link

https://www.youtube.com/watch?time_continue=2&v=hFbBERYN88o

God is love

… God is love; whoever abides in love abides in God, and God in him. (1 John 4:16)

If we do not love we do not have God in us.

Beloved, let us love one another, because love comes from God. Everyone who loves has been born of God and knows God. Whoever does not love does not know God, because God is love. (1 John 4:7-8)

Yes, the Bible tells us what love is.

This is love, that we follow his commandments. This is the commandment, That, as ye have heard from the beginning, ye should follow it. (2 John 1:6)

This is love

This is the love of God, that we keep his commandments: and his commandments are not hard to keep. (1 John 5:3)

… Love me and keep my commandments (Exodus 20:6)

If ye love me, keep my commandments. (John 14:15)

The Sermon on the Mount or The Beatitudes

The Sermon on the Mount or The Beatitudes can be found in

The Gospel of Matthew, chapters 5, 6 and 7.

Give and share

If you have two garments, share with someone that has none and the same with food. (Luke 3:11)

True Love

The greatest way to show love for your friend is by giving your life for them. (John 15:13)

Live like Jesus

Whosoever claims to be like Jesus must live the way He lived. (1 John 2:6)

Law AS WELL AS grace

Are we to obey the Law or accept the grace and   truth?
This truly is a silly question. It is both, of course. How could you have grace if there was no Law?

59

The law was given by Moses; grace and truth came through Jesus Christ. (John 1:17)

Great mercy

He does not treat us as we deserve according to our bad behaviour nor do we get repaid according to our evil deeds. But as high as the heavens are above the earth, so great is His mercy and love towards those that fear and respect Him. (Psalm 103:10-11)

His mercy from generation to generation

His mercy extends to those who fear Him, from generation to generation. (Luke 1:50)

11. Scripture Verses About God's Will

Do God's will and live forever

The world and all its desires is passing away,but anyone who does God's will shall live forever. (1 John 2:17)

Do God's will to be related to Jesus

Whoever does the will of God, is my brother, my sister, and mother. (Mark 3:35)

Teach me to do your will

Teach me to do your will; for thou art my God: thy spirit is good; lead me into the land of uprightness. (Psalm 143:10)

Do my Father's will to enter the kingdom

Not every one that saith unto me, Lord, Lord, shall enter into the kingdom of heaven; but he that does the will of my Father which is in heaven. (Matthew 7:21)

For I have come down from heaven, not to do My own will, but to do the will of Him who sent Me.

And this is the will of Him who sent Me, that I shall lose none of those He has given Me, but raise them up at the last day.

For it is My Father's will that everyone who looks to the Son and believes in Him shall have eternal life, and I will raise him up at the last day. (John 6:38-40)

Do His will to understand the Truth

If any man will do his will, he shall know of the doctrine, whether it be of God, or whether I speak of myself. (John 7:17)

The LORD confides in those who fear Him, and reveals His covenant to them. (Psalm 25:14)

Have God's law in your heart

I delight to do your will, O my God; your law is within my heart. (Psalm 40:8)

God listens to those who do His will

We know that God does not listen to sinners, but if anyone is a worshiper of God and does his will, God listens to him. (John 9:31)

My nourishment comes from doing God's will

Then Jesus said: "My food comes from doing the will of God, who sent me, and from finishing his work." (John 4:34)

God's will written with His own finger

I will give you the tablets with the law and the commandments which I have written on stone

with my own finger for the instruction of my people;

'If ye love me, keep my commandments.' (Exodus 24:12, 31:18, John 14:15)

Is Heaven just for Jesus' friends?

https://liveforeverhowto.wordpress.com/2015/10/2
3/is-heaven-just-for-jesus-
friends/?iframe=true&theme_preview=true   From
Mimi's liveforeverhowto.wordpress.com blog.

12. AFTERWORD

See, hear and consider

So shall he sprinkle many nations. Kings shall be speechless in his presence. For that which had not been told them shall they see; and that which they had not heard shall they consider.(Isaiah 52:15)

Written with the finger of God in stone

And he gave unto Moses, when he had made an end of communing with him upon mount Sinai, two tables of testimony, tables of stone, written with the finger of God. (Exodus 31:18)

Forever settled in heaven

For ever, O LORD, thy word is settled in heaven. (Psalm 119:89)

Keep my Commandments always

O that there were such an heart in them, that they would fear me, and keep all my Commandments always, that it might be well with them, and with their children for ever! (Deuteronomy 5:29)

My words dear within your heart

Hold my words dear within your heart...
"I will put my law in their minds and write it on

their hearts." (Deuteronomy 11:18, Jeremiah 31:33)

Other books by Mimi Emmanuel on health, faith & book publishing

are available from Amazon.com **&** www.mimiemmanuel.com

SHARING FROM HER HEART - "I enjoy Mimi's style of writing. She has a way of drawing the reader in to sit next to her while she wraps her arm around you and tells her tale while you listen." Virginia Ritterbush, #1 Bestselling author of Reframe Your Viewpoints

Mimi lives in Wide Bay, Queensland, Australia in a treehouse overlooking the bay with her family, puppies Layla-Joy, Lilac-Delight, and SweetPea, the rescued magpie..

Lunch is enjoyed with the butcherbirds and geckos, whilst watching the kangaroos with their joeys hop around her front yard.

Mimi was born in Sydney and grew up in Europe. She lived on the beach where she helped her parents in their kiosk. Later on Mimi worked in the medical industry. She burned-out and initiated a career change. Mimi is now living her dream as an author. She writes from her recliner with industrial-strength mufflers on, and this is how she's become a bestselling author with her books ranking #1 bestsellers in over 40 categories.

Mimi is also a popular inspirational speaker. She can be contacted on her website for speaking engagements and private coaching sessions.

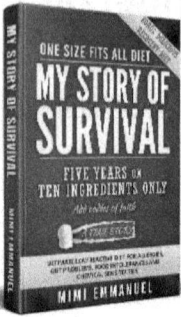

#1 Best Seller ☆☆☆☆☆

MY STORY OF SURVIVAL
THIS IS A GOD-SEND READ!
"This is a God-send read for those with mysterious food intolerances. Mimi learned how to craft her own survival diet out of just a very few ingredients. She shares her journey to show that there are answers to be found." #1 Bestselling author of Toolkit for Wellness - Deidre J Edwards

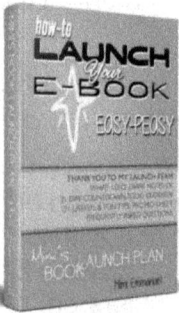

#1 Best Seller ☆☆☆☆☆

MIMI'S BOOK LAUNCH PLAN
SIMPLY BRILLIANT - A WEALTH OF KNOWLEDGE
"Perfect for all writers… the book is well written - it's like having a trusted friend in the same room with you… Highly recommended."
Bestselling author P Patel

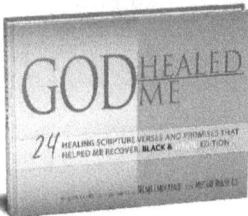

#1 Best Seller ☆☆☆☆☆

GOD HEALED ME
PROMISES THAT MOVE MOUNTAINS
"This is a wonderful book about a woman who was very ill and who overcame her illness by standing daily upon the promises in God's word."

- Wade Howard
Check out the GOD HEALED ME JOURNAL also!

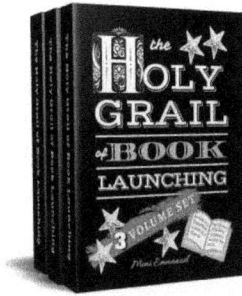

THE HOLY GRAIL OF BOOK LAUNCHING
THIS BOOK IS SOLID GOLD
"This book is a One-Stop Shop for everything you need (or could ever imagine)... nothing is left out!" Dr Gia
"Very generous, comprehensive, user-friendly." Utta Gabbay

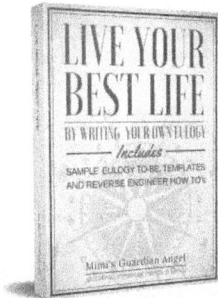

LIVE YOUR BEST LIFE
WOW. THIS BOOK BLEW ME AWAY! "This is a powerful book. This is the type of book that changes your thinking and can change the world!"
#1 Bestselling author of Author Your Success -Ray Breh

The Truth, Love & God series (1)

www.ingramcontent.com/pod-product-compliance
Lightning Source LLC
Chambersburg PA
CBHW071931020426
42331CB00010B/2808